D0641285

Other books in this series:
Women's Quotations   Garden Lover's Quotations
Book Lover's Quotations   Dance Lover's Quotations
Music Lover's Quotations   Friendship Quotations
Art Lover's Quotations

Published simultaneously in 1993 by Exley Publications in
Great Britain, and Exley Giftbooks in the USA.

12   11   10   9   8   7   6

Selection and arrangement © Helen Exley 1993.
Editor Helen Exley

ISBN 1-85015-266-7

Edited by Helen Exley.

Picture research by Image Select International.
Typesetting by Delta, Watford.
Printed in Singapore.

Exley Publications Ltd, 16 Chalk Hill, Watford, Herts
WD1 4BN, United Kingdom.
Exley Publications LLC, 232 Madison Avenue, Suite
1206, NY 10016, USA.

Exley Publications is very grateful to the following individuals for
permission to reproduce their pictures: The Bridgeman Art Library,
cover and title page and pages 6/7, 18, 35, 36/37; © DACS 1993 'Lowry
The Pond' 1950, page 52/53; E T Archive, pages 8, 14/15, 46, 49, 52/53;
Image Bank, pages 11, 12, 16, 21, 23, 24/25, 26/27, 32, 34, 39, 45, 54/55,
56/57; National Railway Museum, York, cover; Scala, pages 28/29,
40/41, 58.

THE BEST OF
BUSINESS
QUOTATIONS

A HELEN EXLEY GIFTBOOK

EXLEY
NEW YORK · WATFORD, UK

"Being good is good business."

ANITA RODDICK, b.1943,
founder and managing director, Body Shop International

"Business is many things, the least of which is the balance sheet. It is a fluid, ever changing, living thing, sometimes building to great peaks, sometimes falling to crumbled lumps. The soul of a business is a curious alchemy of needs, desires, greed and gratifications mixed together with selflessness, sacrifices and personal contributions far beyond material rewards."

HAROLD GENEEN, b.1910,
International Telephone & Telegraph Company

"It horrifies me that ethics is only an optional extra at Harvard Business School."

SIR JOHN HARVEY-JONES, b.1924,
former chairman, Imperial Chemical Industries

"If you do things well, do them better. Be daring, be first, be different, be just."

ANITA RODDICK, b.1943,
founder and managing director, Body Shop International

"Have regard for your name,
since it will remain for
you longer than a great
store of gold."

"The Apocrypha, Ecclesiasticus 41:12"

"If you do anything just for the money you
don't succeed."

BARRY HEARN,
snooker promoter

"We need a fresh vision of business enterprise. In a society that has become predominantly urban and suburban we need a form of work organisation, and a work ethic, that offers men and women a certain scope, a certain dignity and freedom, and not just an existence."

GEORGE GODYER,
British International Paper Ltd

"Top management must know how good or bad employees' working conditions are. They must eat in the employees' restaurants, see whether the food is well cooked, visit the washroom and lavatories. If they are not good enough for those in charge they are not good enough for anyone."

LORD SIEFF (1889 - 1972),
interview, "Sunday Telegraph Magazine"

"If you find a way of working so that people are cared for, they will give of their best, strive for excellence, or at least do better than the competition. That way round you cannot lose. Yes it is about good staff canteens, cloakrooms, pay and pensions. But in the end it is about caring."

SIR HECTOR LANG,
United Biscuits (Holdings)

"Take the loos - I've always believed industrial democracy starts in the lavatory."

SIR PETER PARKER,
then chairman, British Rail

"My formula for success is to be found in three words - work - work - work."

SILVIO BERLUSCONI,
Italian media proprietor

"To be successful, the first thing to do is fall in love with your work."

SISTER MARY LAURETTA,
Roman Catholic nun

"At Amstrad the staff start early and finish late. Nobody takes lunches - they may get a sandwich slung on their desk - there's no small talk. It's all action and the atmosphere is amazing, and the *ésprit de corps* is terrific. Working hard is fun."

ALAN SUGAR, b.1942,
founder and chairman, Amstrad

"To love is to be engaged is to work is to be interested is to create."

LINA WERTMULLER, b.1929,
film maker

"Everything comes to him who hustles while he waits."

THOMAS A. EDISON

"Unless you are willing to drench yourself
in your work beyond the capacity of the
average person, you are just not cut out for
positions at the top."

J. C. PENNEY,
former chairman, J. C. Penney

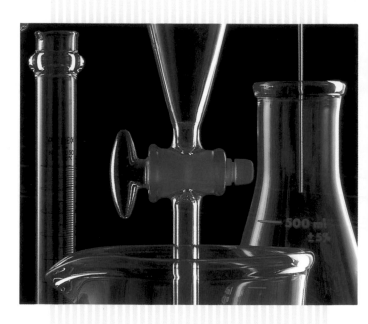

"The only limits are, as always, those of vision."

JAMES BROUGHTON

"Each problem has hidden in it an opportunity so powerful that it literally dwarfs the problem. The greatest success stories were created by people who recognized a problem and turned it into an opportunity."

JOSEPH SUGARMAN

"I'm a mover and a shaker. The movers and shakers are all about change. Not doing things the way they've always been done, or keeping your head below the parapet."

SIR RALPH HALPERN, b.1938,
chairman of British Fashion Council

"And the trouble is, if you don't risk anything, you risk even more."

ERICA JONG, b.1942
writer

"If you see a bandwagon, it's too late."

SIR JAMES GOLDSMITH,
founder of industrial, commercial and financial enterprises

"I want to work for a company that contributes to and is part of the community. I want something not just to invest in. I want something to believe in."

ANITA RODDICK, b.1943,
founder and managing director, Body Shop International

"Management must have a purpose, a dedication and that dedication must have an emotional commitment. It must be built in as a vital part of the personality of anyone who truly is a manager."

HAROLD GENEEN, b.1910,
International Telephone & Telegraph Company

"If you don't know where you are going, you will probably end up somewhere else."

DR. LAURENCE J. PETER, b.1919,
Canadian educator

"If one wants to be successful, one must think; one must think until it hurts. One must worry a problem in one's mind until it seems there cannot be another aspect of it that hasn't been considered."

LORD THOMSON OF FLEET (1894 - 1976),
former chairman, Thomson Organisation

"If there's a way to do it better . . . find it."

THOMAS A. EDISON

"You see things; and you say, 'Why?' But I dream things that never were; and I say, 'Why not?'."

GEORGE BERNARD SHAW (1856-1950),
Irish dramatist

"Always bear in mind that your own resolution to succeed is more important than any other one thing."

ABRAHAM LINCOLN

"In business, if you are persistent you normally arrive. It's the old tortoise and hare story."

NOEL LISTER,
co-founder and former chief executive, MFI Furniture Group

"Most people give up just when they're about to achieve success.
They quit on the one yard line. They give up at the last minute of the game one foot from a winning touch."

H. ROSS PEROT, b.1930,
business executive and politician

"Many people dream of success. To me success can only be achieved through repeated failure and introspection. In fact, success represents 1% of your work which results from the 99% that is called failure."

SOICHIRO HONDA, b.1906,
founder, Honda Corporation

"Few things are impossible to diligence and skill...Great works are performed not by strength, but perseverence."

SAMUEL JOHNSON (1709-1784),
writer

"Procrastination is opportunity's natural assassin."

VICTOR KIAM,
president and chief executive, Remington Products Inc.

"Work expands so as to fill the time available for its completion."

PROFESSOR C. NORTHCOTE PARKINSON (1909-1993),
author "Parkinson's Law"

"Well we can't stand here doin' nothing, people will think we're workmen."

SPIKE MILLIGAN, b.1918,
British comedian

"While you're negotiating for a 35 hour week, remember they have only just got 66 hours in Taiwan, and you're competing with Taiwan."

VICTOR KIAM,
president and chief executive officer, Remington Products Inc.

"An enterprise culture is one in which every individual understands that the world does not owe him or her a living."

PETER MORGAN, b.1936,
director general, Institute of Directors

"The freedom to fail is vital if you're going to succeed. Most successful people fail time and time again, and it is a measure of their strength that failure merely propels them into some new attempt at success."

MICHAEL KORDA

"If you have made mistakes...there is always another chance for you...you may have a fresh start any moment you choose, for this thing we call 'failure' is not the falling down, but the staying down."

MARY PICKFORD (1893-1979),
actress

"...You may be disappointed if you fail, but you are doomed if you don't try."

BEVERLY SILLS, b.1929,
opera singer and manager

"Never accept failure, no matter how often it visits you.
Keep on going. Never give up. Never."

DR. MICHAEL SMURFIT,
Jefferson Smurfit

"The quality of a person's life is in direct
proportion to their commitment to
excellence, regardless of their chosen field
of endeavour."

VINCENT T. LOMBARDI

"I think it is an immutable law in business
that words are words, explanations are
explanations, promises are promises - but
only performance is reality."

HAROLD GENEEN, b.1910,
former chief executive,
International Telephone & Telegraph Company

"It is my profound belief that a man or woman who rises up through the hierarchy of a corporation must justify his or her position every single day. They must also be in a state of perpetual anxiety, the healthy anxiety that makes one reject complacency."

JACQUES MAISONROUGE,
former senior vice-president, IBM

"Contrary to the cliché, genuinely nice guys most often finish first or very near it."

MALCOLM FORBES (1919 - 1990),
publisher

"The man who is denied the opportunity of taking decisions of importance begins to regard as important the decisions he is allowed to take. He becomes fussy about filing, keen on seeing pencils are

sharpened, eager to ensure that the
windows are opened (or shut) and apt to
use two or three different coloured
pencils."

PROFESSOR C. NORTHCOTE PARKINSON, (1909-1993),

"Selling has to be the most exciting thing you can do with your clothes on."

JOHN FENTON,
guru

"It really gets my adrenalin flowing to hear the ping of the cash registers."

STANLEY KALMS, b.1931

"I have no private life. I have a wife who understands.
When the phone doesn't ring at home I get depressed. So my wife says, 'Why not go out and sell something, Lew?' And that always cheers me up."

LORD GRADE, b.1906,
television mogul

"Always do your best. What you plant
now, you will harvest later."
O. G. MANDINO

"It is not the employer who pays wages; he
only handles the money. It is the product
that pays wages."
HENRY FORD (1863-1947),
American automobile engineer and manufacturer

"Hard work never killed a man. Men die
of boredom, psychological conflict and
disease. Indeed the harder your people
work, the happier and healthier
they will be."
DAVID OGILVY, b.1911,
founder, Ogilvy and Mather

"Life is to be lived. If you have to support
yourself, you had bloody well better find
some way that is going to be interesting.
And you don't do that by sitting around."
KATHARINE HEPBURN, b.1909,
actress

"The only place where success comes
before work is in the dictionary."
VIDAL SASSOON, b.1928,
hair stylist

"What I am trying to do is communicate harmony of interest between the company and the staff. We are not adversaries. We are partners."

SIR HECTOR LANG,
United Biscuits (Holdings)

"Our experience proves that a policy of good human relations results in self-discipline, staff stability, good service to the customer, high productivity and good profits in which we all share: employees, shareholders, pensioners and the community."

LORD SIEFF (1889 - 1972),
former chairman Marks & Spencer

"It is the responsibility of the leadership and the management to give opportunities and put demands on people which enable them to grow as human beings in their work environment."

SIR JOHN HARVEY-JONES, b.1924

"The worst mistake a boss can make is not to say 'well done'."

JOHN ASHCROFT, b.1948
former chairman, Coloroll

"The bigger the headquarters the more decadent the company."

SIR JAMES GOLDSMITH,
founder and proprietor of a number of industrial and financial enterprises

"The more luxurious the luncheon rooms at headquarters, the more inefficient the business."

ROLAND FRANKLIN,
founder, Pembridge Investments

"All these ego-feeding activities - the long hours in the limousine, the sky-larking in the corporate jet, the collection of press clippings, the unnecessary speeches - feed the corporate sickness and one way or another make a corporate problem out of what had been an otherwise perfectly competent, even brilliant executive."

HAROLD GENEEN, b.1910,
*former chief executive,
International Telephone & Telegraph Company*

"If you want a place in the sun you've got to put up with a few blisters."

ABIGAIL VAN BUREN, b.1918,
American writer and journalist

"The person who is devoted to paperwork
has lost the initiative. He is dealing with
things that are brought to his notice,
having ceased to notice anything for
himself. He has been essentially defeated
in his job."

PROFESSOR C. NORTHCOTE PARKINSON (1909 - 1993),
author "Parkinson's Law"

"In a hierarchy every employee tends to rise to his level of incompetence."
DR. LAURENCE J. PETER, b.1919

"It is not the crook in modern business that we fear, but the honest man who doesn't know what he is doing."
OWEN D. YOUNG

"I believe that crisis really tends to help develop the character of an organisation."

JOHN SCULLEY,
president, Apple Computer Inc.

"I need problems. A good problem makes me come alive."

"TINY" ROLAND,
chief executive, Lonrho

"An overburdened, stretched executive is the best executive, because he or she doesn't have time to meddle, to deal in trivia, to bother people."

JACK WELCH,
chairman, US General Electric

"I don't know any executive who ever thought about stress, although a lot of other people do. No one ever dies of hard work. But a lot of people die once they retire from an active job."

SIR IAN MACGREGOR, b.1912,
former chairman, National Coal Board

"I enjoy pressure, can't do without it."

GEORGE DAVIES,
then chairman, Next

"To get something done a committee should consist of no more than three people, two of whom are absent."
ROBERT COPELAND

"A conference is a gathering of important people who singly can do nothing, but together can decide that nothing can be done."

FRED ALLEN (John F. Sullivan) (1894 - 1956),
American comedian

"When money is at stake, never be the first to mention sums."

SHEIKH AHMED YAMANI, b.1930,
former Saudi Arabian oil minister

"The secret of business is knowing something that nobody else knows."

ARISTOTLE ONASSIS (1906 - 1975),
shipping tycoon

"To be successful, keep looking tanned, live in an elegant building (even if you're in the cellar), be seen in smart restaurants (even if you nurse one drink) and if you borrow, borrow big."

ARISTOTLE ONASSIS (1906 - 1975),
shipping tycoon

"Corporation: An ingenious device for obtaining individual profit without individual responsibility."

AMBROSE BIERCE (1842 - 1914),
American journalist

"A consultant is someone who saves his client almost enough to pay his fee."

ARNOLD H. GLASOW

"Consultants are people who come down from the hill to shoot the wounded after the battle is over."

DOC BLAKELEY

"I come from an environment where, if you see a snake, you kill it. At General Motors, if you see a snake, the first thing you do is hire a consultant on snakes."

H. ROSS PEROT, b.1930,
former director, General Motors

"When a person with experience meets a person with money, the person with experience will get the money. And the person with money will get some experience."

LEONARD LAUDER

"Business is Darwinism: only the fittest survive."

ROBERT HOLMES À COURT,
Bell Group International

"British Airways has a Jumbo jet simulator, and landing it is exciting and dramatic. But think of being in a real Jumbo, with the pilot slumped dead beside you. That's the real element of life and death. That's what you get in business."

ADAM FAITH,
former pop singer and businessman

"Innovation comes from creative destruction."

YOSHIHISA TABUCHI,
president and chief executive, Normura Securities

"Make sure you have a Vice President in charge of Revolution, to engender ferment among your more conventional colleagues."

DAVID OGILVY, b.1911,
founder Ogilvy and Mather

"All things being equal, people will buy from a friend. All things being not quite so equal, people will *still* buy from a friend."

MARK MCCORMACK, b.1930,
chairman and chief executive officer,
International Management Group

"What matters is working with a few close friends, people you respect, knowing that if times did turn bad these people would hold together."

RICHARD BRANSON, b.1950,
founder and chairman, Virgin Group

"We shall not perish as a people even if we get our money supply wrong - but if we get our human relationships wrong, we shall destroy ourselves."

RT. REVEREND ROBERT RUNCIE, b.1921,
then Archbishop of Canterbury

"Personal wealth has never been important to me. What is important is the team of people I work with."

GEORGE DAVIES,
then chairman, Next

"We treat employees as a member of the family. If management take the risk of hiring them, we have to take the responsibility for them."

AKIO MORITA, b.1921,
chairman and chief executive, Sony Corporation

"Start with good people, lay out the rules, communicate with your employees, motivate them and reward them. If you do all those things effectively, you can't miss."

LEE IACOCCA, b.1924,
Chrysler Corporation

"There is an English proverb that says 'there are no bad students, only bad teachers'. I believe it also applies to a company. There are no bad employees, only bad managers."

T. S. LIN,
Tatung Co.

"First, make yourself a reputation for being a creative genius. Second, surround yourself with partners who are better than you are. Third, leave them to get on with it."

DAVID OGILVY, b.1911,
Ogilvy & Mather

"There's a saying in the United States that the customer is king. But in Japan the customer is God."

TAK KIMOTO,
Sumitronics Inc.

"The absolute fundamental aim is to make money out of satisfying customers."

SIR JOHN EGAN, b.1939,
Jaguar

"We should never be allowed to forget that it is the customer who, in the end, determines how many people are employed and what sort of wages companies can afford."

LORD ROBENS, b.1910,
National Coal Board

"Better service for the customer is for the good of the public, and this is the true purpose of enterprise."

KONOSUKE MATSUSHITA,
founder Matsushita Electric

"Quality is remembered long after the price is forgotten."

Gucci family slogan

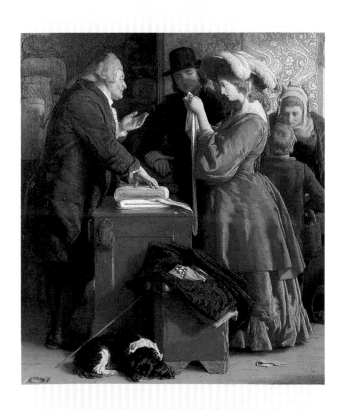

"You must deodorise profits and make people understand that profit is not something offensive, but as important to a company as breathing."

SIR PETER PARKER, b.1924,
then chairman, British Rail

"Creation of wealth is almost a duty because of the widespread benefits that flow from it."

JOHN GUNN,
chief executive, British & Commonwealth plc

"The purpose of industry is to create
wealth. It is not, despite belief to the
contrary, to create jobs. The jobs are
created from the wealth that industry
produces."

SIR JOHN HARVEY-JONES, b.1924,
former chairman, Imperial Chemical Industries

"Making money doesn't oblige people to
forfeit their honor or their conscience."

BARON GUY DE ROTHSCHILD,
banking magnate

"Making money is art and working is art
and good business is the best art of all."

ANDY WARHOL (1926 - 1987),
artist

"Business, more than any other occupation,
is a continual calculation, an instinctive
exercise in foresight."

HENRY R. LUCE (1898 - 1967),
founder, "Time" and "Fortune" magazines

"Business is like sex. When it's good, it's very, very good; when it's not so good, it's still good."

GEORGE KATONA

"I've got a great ambition to die of exhaustion rather than boredom."

ANGUS GROSSART,
Noble Grossart

"The best leaders are apt to be found among those executives who have a strong component of unorthodoxy in their characters. Instead of resisting innovation, they symbolize it - and companies cannot grow without innovation."

DAVID OGILVY, b.1911,
founder, Ogilvy and Mather

"Leaders must be seen to be up front, up to date, up to their job and up early in the morning."

LORD SIEFF (1889 - 1972),
former chairman, Marks & Spencer

"Strategic leadership requires one other skill. It is a readiness to look personally foolish; a readiness to discuss half-baked ideas, since most fully baked ideas start out in that form; a total honesty, a readiness to admit you got it wrong."

SIR JOHN HOSKYNS, b.1927,
Burton Group

"Your legacy should be that you made it better than it was when you got it."

LEE IACOCCA, b.1924,
chairman and chief executive, Chrysler Corporation

"A race horse that can run a mile a few seconds faster is worth twice as much. That little extra proves to be the greatest value."
JOHN D. HESS

"One machine can do the work of fifty ordinary men. No machine can do the work of one extraordinary man."
ELBERT (GREEN) HUBBARD (1856 - 1915),
American businessman, writer and printer

"The people who get on in this world are the people who get up and look for the circumstances they want, and, if they can't find them, make them."
GEORGE BERNARD SHAW (1856-1950),
Irish dramatist

"The kind of people I look for to fill top management spots are the eager beavers, the mavericks. These are the guys who try to do more than they're expected to do – they always reach."
LEE IACOCCA,
Chrysler Corporation